creative new
QUILTS & PROJECTS
from precuts or stash

by Wendy Sheppard

Landauer Publishing, LLC

creative new
QUILTS & PROJECTS
from precuts or stash

Copyright © 2015 by Landauer Publishing, LLC

Projects Copyright © 2015
by Wendy Sheppard

This book was designed, produced,
and published by Landauer Publishing, LLC
3100 101st Street, Urbandale, IA 50322
www.landauerpub.com
515/287/2144 800/557/2144

President/Publisher: Jeramy Lanigan Landauer

Editor: Jeri Simon

Art Director: Laurel Albright

Photographer: Sue Voegtlin

Library of Congress Control Number: 2015939382
ISBN 13: 978-1-935726-75-3
This book printed on acid-free paper.
Printed in United States
10-9-8-7-6-5-4-3-2-1

 FACEBOOK.COM/
LANDAUERPUBLISHING
 YOUTUBE.COM/
LANDAUERPUBLISHING
 PINTEREST.COM/
LANDAUERPUB

contents

dedication

Dedicated to my six-year-old daughter, Gwendolyn, who has discovered the joy of needle and thread since my first book *Recreating Antique Quilts*. She has become my fast and best stitching buddy.

Gwendolyn's Dream Garden
QUILT

introduction

Precut fabric bundles are one of the biggest buzzes in the quilting world. The major draw to these convenient bundles is they are conducive to fast and easy cutting for the quick completion of quilt projects. In addition to being creatively packaged, they also give quilters a chance to enjoy all the fabrics in one line. More fabrics automatically means scrappier quilts, and we all know how delightfully obsessive we quilters are with scrappy quilts.

I have a small cutting area. Working with precut fabrics is very convenient for me. I always tend to cut my non-precut fabrics into smaller, more manageable pieces before I start cutting pieces for my quilt projects. Precuts always save me a few extra steps in cutting, especially the 2-1/2" strips which I love to use to make my binding strips.

Precuts from your stash

There is no written rule that says you have to use all the precut fabric pieces within a bundle. In fact, most quilt projects will NOT use every fabric in the bundle. You will end up with precut pieces in your fabric stash, so why not store your leftover precut pieces for future projects? I have heard from many quilters who cut their leftover fabrics into convenient sizes, store and label them to make their own precut fabric stash. What a fantastic idea! Some of the projects in this book were made with precut scraps from my stash.

In *Creative New Quilts & Projects from Precuts or Stash*, I have sought to interject more design elements as well as possibilities into precuts projects.

I attempted to keep the projects non-fabric specific, which makes personalizing the quilt projects so much easier and fun. If fabric lines were used, the names are listed in the project instructions, but quilters can easily pull leftovers from previous precut bundles for any of the projects. The fabrics listed in the instructions can easily be changed, based on what you have in your stash. For example, when a fat quarter is listed in the supplies list, substitute with a variety of 5" or 10" squares.

Changing the size of the projects

The projects in this book offer a variety of sizes, from a hanging banner to a bed quilt. However, each project can easily be made larger or smaller by either changing the block size or the number of blocks. For example, Counting My Blessings on page 30 can easily be enlarged by adding more or wider strips to the quilt top.

There are a few simple appliqué projects included to illustrate that precuts are versatile for any type of project. While many quilters use scraps to add a multitude of colors to their appliqué projects, I treat the small precut fabrics as "scraps" when I audition fabrics for my appliqué projects.

Precut fabric bundles have brought such fun and excitement to quilters, and I believe they will continue to do so for a long time. With that in mind, it is my hope that you will enjoy using your precut bundles to make the projects in *Creative New Quilts & Projects from Precuts or Stash*.

Quiltingly yours,
Wendy Sheppard

Fat Quarter 18" x 22" piece of fabric	Fat Eighth 9" x 22" piece of fabric
2-1/2" x WOF Strips Common names: Jelly Roll, Roll Ups, Pops, Rolie Polies, Pixie Strips, Strips	5" Fabric Squares Common names: Charms, Snaps, Minis, 5" Stackers, Chips, Stamps
10" Fabric Squares Common names: Layer Cakes, Crackers, Ten Squares, Patty Cakes, Squares, 10" Stackers, Tiles, Stacks	Triangles Common names: Turnovers, HST (half-square triangles)
1-1/2" x WOF Strips Common names: Honey Buns, Skinny Strips, Rolie Polies	2-1/2" Squares Common names: Candies, Mini Charms
5" x 44" Strips Common names: Dessert Roll, Twice the Charm, Fat Rolls, Charm Rolls	6" Hexagons Common names: Hexies, Honeycombs

Crossings Quilt

Designed, pieced and quilted by Wendy Sheppard
Finished block size: 12" square
Finished quilt size approximately: 54" x 60"

Materials

Note: I used a group of tonal color fat quarters for the featured quilt. For a scrappier look, use a large assortment of fat quarters in a variety of prints.

2 red tonal fat quarters

1 dark brown tonal fat quarter

2 light brown tonal fat quarters

2 green tonal fat quarters

2 yellow tonal fat quarters

2 lime tonal fat quarters

1 pink tonal fat quarter

1 orange tonal fat quarter

1 royal blue tonal fat quarter

1 aqua tonal fat quarter

1 light blue tonal fat quarter

2-1/2 yards pale gray tonal fabric

3/4 yard white solid fabric

60" x 72" batting

60" x 72" backing fabric

(7) 2-1/2" x wof assorted tonal strips

Fat quarter = 18" x 22"
wof = width of fabric
Sew with a 1/4" seam unless otherwise noted.

Cutting Instructions

From red tonal fat quarters, cut:
(20) 5" squares

From dark brown tonal fat quarter, cut:
(20) 1-1/2" x 5" rectangles

From light brown tonal fat quarters, cut:
(40) 1-1/2" x 5" rectangles
(20) 1-1/2" squares

From green tonal fat quarters, cut:
(16) 5" squares

From yellow tonal fat quarters, cut:
(16) 5" squares

From lime tonal fat quarters, cut:
(16) 5" squares

From pink tonal fat quarter, cut:
(32) 1-1/2" x 5" rectangles
(16) 1-1/2" squares

From orange tonal fat quarter, cut:
(32) 1-1/2" x 5" rectangles
(16) 1-1/2" squares

From royal blue tonal fat quarter, cut:
(32) 1-1/2" x 5" rectangles
(16) 1-1/2" squares

From aqua tonal fat quarter, cut:
(12) 5" squares

From light blue tonal fat quarter, cut:
(24) 1-1/2" x 5" rectangles
(12) 1-1/2" squares

From pale gray tonal fabric, cut:
(8) 2" x wof strips. From the strips, cut: (160) 2" squares
(14) 3-1/2" x wof strips. From the strips, cut:
    (160) 3-1/2" squares

(6) 3-1/2" x wof strips. Piece the strips together and cut:
    (2) 3-1/2" x 54-1/2" top/bottom outer border strips
    (2) 3-1/2" x 60-1/2" side outer border strips

From white solid fabric, cut:
(13) 1-1/2" x wof strips. From the strips, cut:
    (40) 1-1/2" squares
    (20) 1-1/2" x 3-1/2" rectangles
    (60) 1-1/2" x 5-1/2" rectangles

Block Assembly

Note: Set aside the trimmed triangles to make the Flight of Colors Pillow on page 60.

1. Draw a diagonal line on the wrong side of a 3-1/2" pale gray tonal square. With right sides together, place the marked square on a corner of a 5" yellow tonal square.

2. Stitch on drawn line. Trim 1/4" away from sewn line. Press open to reveal the pale gray corner triangle. Repeat on the opposite corner of the yellow tonal square to complete a corner unit. Make 4 corner units.

Make 4

3. Sew 1-1/2" orange tonal squares to opposite sides of a 1-1/2" white solid square to make a block row. Make 2 block rows.

Make 2

4. Sew the block rows to opposite sides of a 1-1/2" x 3-1/2" white solid rectangle to complete a block center.

5. Sew 1-1/2" x 5-1/2" orange tonal rectangles to opposite sides of 1-1/2" x 5-1/2" white solid rectangle.

6. Draw a diagonal line on the wrong side of a 2" pale gray tonal square. With right sides together, place a marked square on the corner of the unit in step 5.

7. Stitch on drawn line. Trim 1/4" away from sewn line. Press open to reveal the pale gray tonal corner triangle. Repeat on the adjacent corner to complete a cross unit. Make 4 cross units.

Make 4

8. Sew 2 cross units to opposite sides of the block center to make the center block row.

9. Sew 2 corner units to opposite sides of a cross unit to make a block row. Make 2 block rows.

10. Sew the block rows to opposite sides of the center block row to complete the cross block.

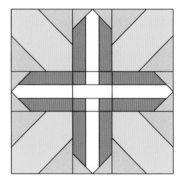

11. Make 20 cross blocks in the following numbers and colorways.

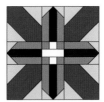

5 blocks

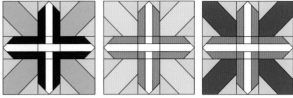

4 blocks in each colorway

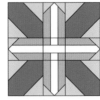

3 blocks

Quilt Top Assembly

1. Referring to the Row Assembly Diagram, lay out the blocks in 5 rows with 4 blocks in each row.

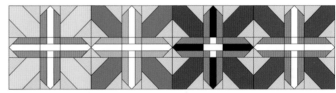

Row 1

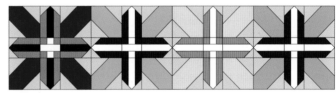

Row 2

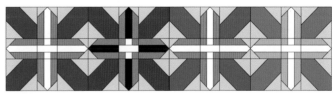

Row 3

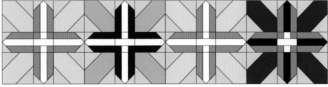

Row 4

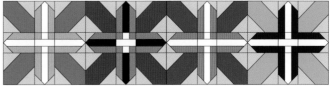

Row 5

Row Assembly Diagram

2. Sew the blocks together in each row. Sew the rows together to complete the quilt center.

3. Sew 3-1/2" x 60-1/2" pale gray tonal side outer border strips to opposite sides of the quilt center.

4. Sew 3-1/2" x 54-1/2" pale gray tonal top/bottom outer border strips to the top and bottom of the quilt center to complete the quilt top.

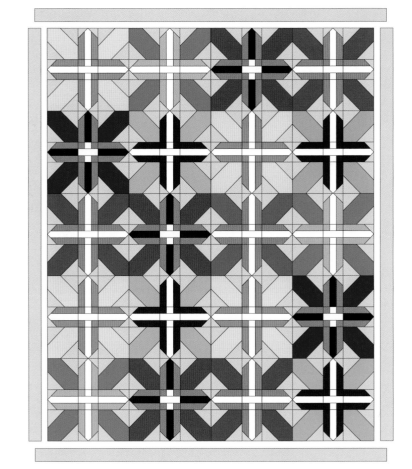

Finishing

1. Lay the backing fabric, wrong side up on a flat surface. The backing fabric should be taut. Place the batting on the backing and the quilt top on the batting, right side up, to form a quilt sandwich. Baste the quilt sandwich.

2. Quilt as desired.

   Quilting notes: *Allover roundabout feather wreaths were quilted over the entire quilt top.*

3. Sew the (7) 2-1/2" x wof binding strips together along the short ends to make one continuous binding strip. Fold the piece in half lengthwise, wrong sides together, and press. Sew to the raw edge of the quilt top. Fold the binding over the raw edges and hand stitch in place on back of quilt.

Roundabout Feather Wreath Quilting Design

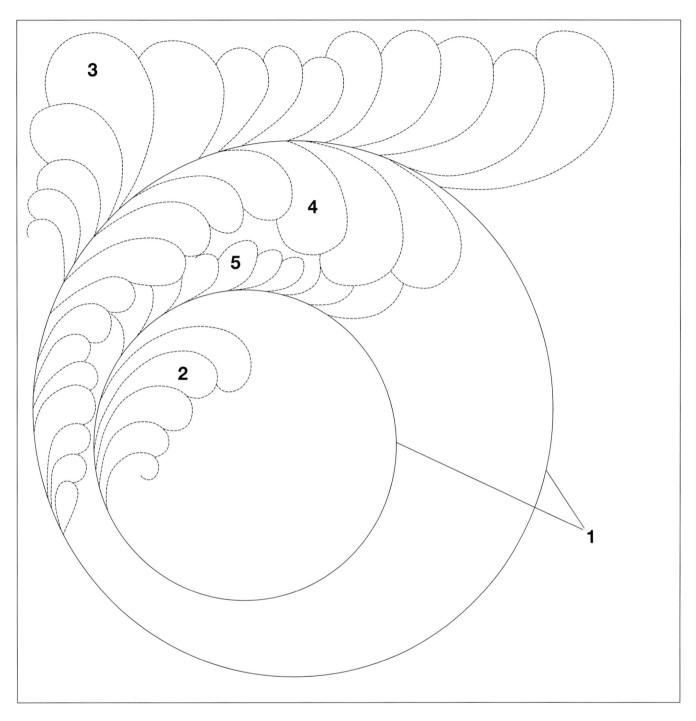

1. Lightly draw the two circles.

2. Quilt feathers in innermost ring.

3. Quilt feathers in outermost ring.

4. Mirror feathers in outermost ring. These feathers are often quilted in such a way that they appear to overlap.

5. Mirror feathers in innermost ring.

Birds of a Feather
PLACE MATS

Designed, pieced and quilted by Wendy Sheppard
Finished place mat size: 16-1/2" x 12"

Materials

Makes 2 place mats

Note: I used The Sweet Life by Pat Sloan for Moda

1 fat quarter focal fabric

1 jelly roll bundle OR
an assortment of (18) 2-1/2" x wof strips

Note: If using a jelly roll bundle, you will have enough strips left to make another set of place mats and the table runner project on page 16.

2 fat quarters backing fabric

(2) 16" x 20" pieces batting

Optional appliqué: 3 fat quarters

Note: There is enough fabric for the appliqués on the place mats and table runner project on page 16.

Fat Quarter = 18" x 22"
Jelly Roll strip = 2-1/2" x wof
wof = width of fabric
Sew with 1/4" seam allowance unless otherwise noted.

Cutting Instructions

From focal fabric fat quarter, cut:
(2) 10-1/2" x 12-1/2" rectangles

From (2) assorted 2-1/2" wof strips, cut:
(4) 1-1/4" x 12-1/2" sashing rectangles

From assorted 2-1/2" wof strips, cut:
(12) 2-1/2" x 5-1/2" rectangles

From 3 fat quarters for optional appliqué, cut:
Appliqué shapes using the templates on page 14

Place Mat Assembly

1. Sew (6) 2-1/2" x 5-1/2" assorted rectangles together along the long edges to make a column.

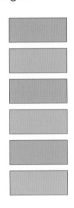

2. Sew (2) 1-1/4" x 12-1/2" sashing rectangles together along one long edge.

3. Sew the sashing rectangles from step 2 to the right side of the column from step 1.

4. Sew a 10-1/2" x 12-1/2" focal fabric rectangle to the remaining side of the sashing rectangle to complete one place mat top.

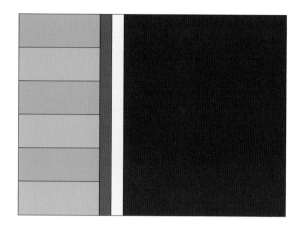

Optional Appliqué: Prepare the appliqué shapes using your favorite method. Fusible appliqué was used on the featured place mats. Referring to the diagrams and the photo on page 15, arrange the prepared appliqué pieces on the place mat top. Sew the pieces in place using a favorite appliqué stitch.

5. Lay the backing fabric, wrong side up on a flat surface. The backing fabric should be taut. Layer batting and place mat top, right side up, on top of backing to form a sandwich. Baste the sandwich.

6. Quilt as desired.

7. Sew (2) 2-1/2" x wof strips together along the short ends to make one continuous strip for binding. Fold the piece in half lengthwise, wrong sides together, and press. Sew to the raw edge of the place mat top. Fold the binding over the raw edges and hand stitch in place on back of place mat.

8. Repeat the steps to make another place mat.

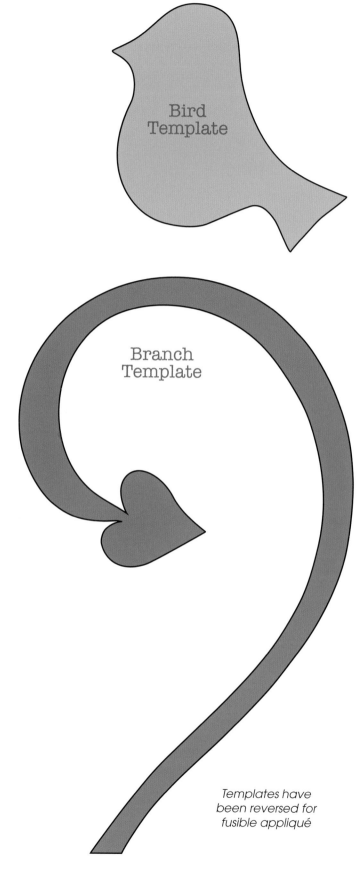

Bird Template

Branch Template

Templates have been reversed for fusible appliqué

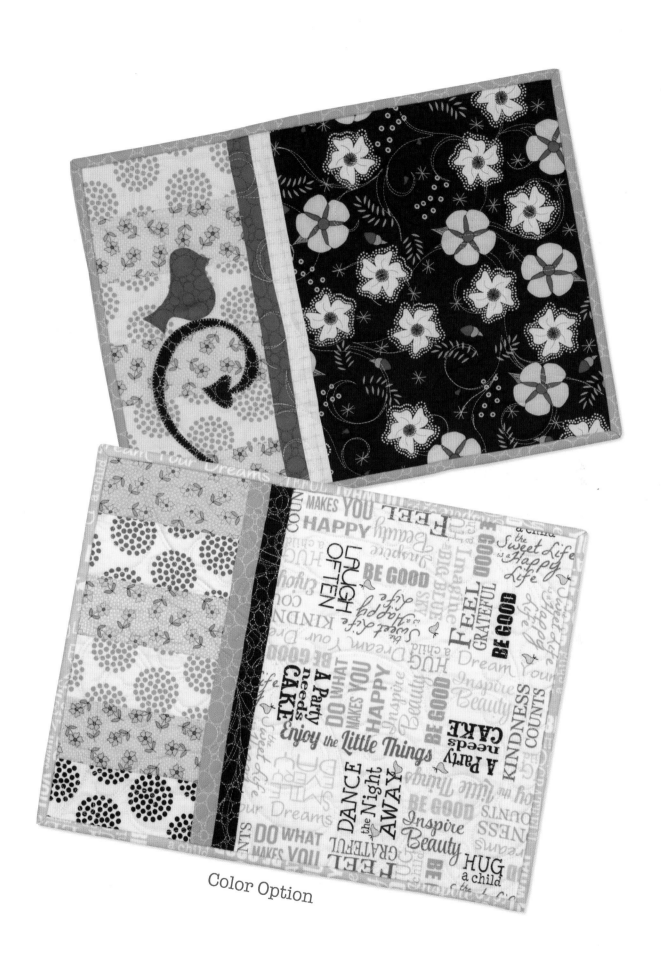

Color Option

Birds of a Feather
TABLE RUNNER

Designed, pieced and quilted by Wendy Sheppard
Finished table runner size approximately: 41" x 15"

Materials

Note: I used The Sweet Life by Pat Sloan for Moda

Note: If you made the place mats on page 12, use the leftover jelly roll strips to make the table runner.

1 fat quarter yellow floral fabric

1 fat quarter aqua floral fabric

1 fat quarter aqua small floral fabric

1 fat quarter green dot on beige fabric

1 fat quarter gray word fabric

1 fat quarter beige tonal fabric

1 fat quarter yellow small floral fabric

(1) 2-1/2" x wof gray small floral strip

(1) 2-1/2" x wof aqua small floral strip

(1) 2-1/2" x wof gray tonal strip

(4) 2-1/2" x wof binding strips

2 fat quarters backing fabric

46" x 20" batting

Optional appliqué: 3 fat quarters

Note: There is enough fabric for the appliqués on the table runner and the place mats on page 12.

Fat Quarter = 18" x 22"
wof = width of fabric
Sew with 1/4" seam allowance unless otherwise noted.

Cutting Instructions

From yellow floral fat quarter, cut:
(1) 8-1/2" x 15-1/2" rectangle

From aqua floral fat quarter, cut:
(1) 7-1/2" x 15-1/2" rectangle

From aqua small floral fat quarter, cut:
(12) 3" squares

From green dot on beige fat quarter, cut:
(12) 3" squares

From gray word fat quarter, cut:
(24) 1-3/4" squares
(1) 3-1/2" x 15-1/2" rectangle

From beige tonal fat quarter, cut:
(24) 1-3/4" squares
(3) 1-1/2" x 15-1/2" sashing rectangles

From yellow small floral fat quarter, cut:
(1) 3-1/2" x 15-1/2" rectangle

From gray small floral strip, cut:
(1) 2-1/2" x 15-1/2" rectangle

From aqua small floral strip, cut:
(1) 2-1/2" x 15-1/2" rectangle

From gray tonal strip, cut:
(4) 1-1/4" x 15-1/2" sashing rectangles

From 3 fat quarters for optional appliqué, cut:
Appliqué shapes using the bird template on page 14 and the branch templates on page 21

Block Assembly

1. Draw a diagonal line on the wrong side of the 1-3/4" gray word squares. With right sides together, place a marked square on one corner of a 3" aqua small floral square.

2. Sew on the drawn line. Trim 1/4" away from the sewn line. Press the triangle open.

3. Repeat on the opposite corner of the aqua small floral square to make a gray/aqua subunit. Make a total of 12 gray/aqua subunits.

Make 12

4. Draw a diagonal line on the wrong side of the 1-3/4" beige tonal squares. With right sides together, place a marked square on one corner of a 3" green dot on beige square.

5. Sew on the drawn line. Trim 1/4" away from the sewn line. Press the triangle open.

6. Repeat on the opposite corner of the green dot on beige square to make a beige/green dot subunit. Make a total of 12 beige/green dot subunits.

Make 12

7. Lay out 2 gray/aqua subunits and 2 beige/green dot subunits as shown. Sew the subunits together in pairs.

8. Sew the pairs together to make a block. Make a total of 6 blocks.

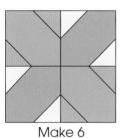

Make 6

Table Runner Assembly

1. Lay out 3 blocks in a vertical row as shown. Sew the blocks together to make a block column. Make a total of 2 block columns.

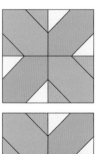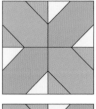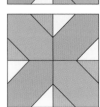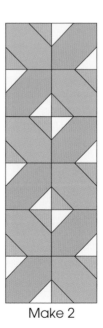

Make 2

2. Referring to the Table Runner Assembly Diagram, lay out 2 block columns, (4) 1-1/4" x 15-1/2" gray tonal sashing rectangles, (1) 2-1/2" x 15-1/2" aqua small floral rectangle, (1) 3-1/2" x 15-1/2" yellow small floral rectangle, (3) 1-1/2" x 15-1/2" beige tonal sashing rectangles, (1) 3-1/2" x 15-1/2" gray word rectangle, (1) 7-1/2" x 15-1/2" aqua focal floral rectangle, (1) 8-1/2" x 15-1/2" yellow focal floral rectangle and (1) 2-1/2" x 15-1/2" gray small floral rectangle as shown.

3. Sew the pieces together to complete the table runner top.

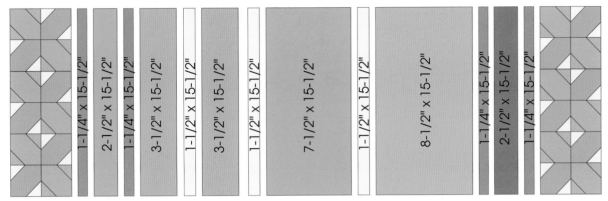

Table Runner Assembly Diagram

Placement Diagram

Optional Appliqué: Prepare the appliqué shapes using your favorite method. Fusible appliqué was used on the table runner. Referring to the placement diagram on page 19, arrange the prepared appliqué pieces on the table runner top. Sew the pieces in place using a favorite appliqué stitch.

Finishing

1. Sew the 2 backing fat quarters together along one short edge.

2. Lay the backing, wrong side up on a flat surface. The backing fabric should be taut. Layer batting and place mat top, right side up, on top of backing to form a sandwich. Baste the sandwich.

3. Quilt as desired.

4. Sew (4) 2-1/2" x wof binding strips together along the short ends to make one continuous strip. Fold the piece in half lengthwise, wrong sides together, and press. Sew to the raw edge of the table runner top. Fold the binding over the raw edges and hand stitch in place on back of table runner.

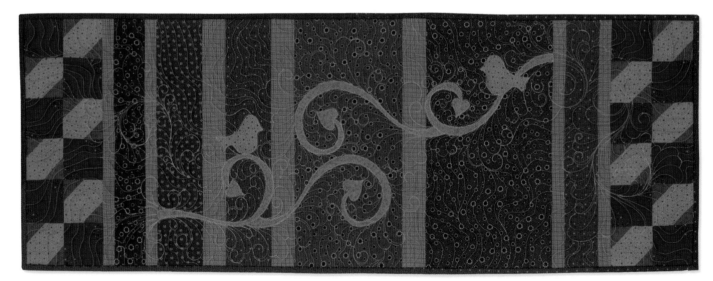

Color Option

Short Branch
Template

Long Branch
Template

Winter Blues
QUILT

Designed, pieced and quilted by Wendy Sheppard
Finished quilt size approximately: 51" x 58-1/2"
Finished block size: 4" x 8"
Finished connecting block size: 2" x 8"

Materials

Note: I used a precut 10" stack of Island Batik Blue Moon fabrics. For a scrappier look, use more than the number of fabric squares given.

13 or more 10" squares of assorted light
  and medium blue fabric

5 or more 10" squares of assorted dark blue fabric

5/8 yard gray crackle print fabric

2-1/8 yards white tonal fabric

1/2 yard light blue fabric

56" x 65" backing fabric

56" x 65" batting

wof = width of fabric
Sew with 1/4" seam allowance unless otherwise noted.

Cutting Instructions

From assorted light and medium blue 10" squares, cut:

(11) 4-1/2" x 8-1/2" rectangles for Block A

(26) 4-1/2" squares for Block B

From assorted dark blue 10" squares, cut:

(22) 2" x 4-1/2" rectangles for Block C

(42) 1-1/2" x 2-1/2" rectangles for Connecting Blocks

(12) 1-1/2" squares for Half-Connecting Blocks

Note: The featured quilt uses identical fabrics for Block C and Connecting Blocks to create a "connecting" effect.

From gray crackle print fabric, cut:

(3) 2-1/2" x wof strips. From the strips, cut:

   (28) 2-1/2" x 4-1/2" rectangles for Block B

(2) 4" x wof strips. From the strips, cut:

   (46) 1-1/2" x 4" rectangles for Connecting and

Half-Connecting Blocks

From white tonal fabric, cut:

(5) 4-1/2" x wof strips.

   From 2 strips, cut:

   (24) 2-1/2" x 4-1/2" rectangles for Block B

   From 3 strips, cut:

   (22) 2-1/2" x 4-1/2" rectangles for Block C and

   (11) 1-1/2" x 4-1/2" rectangles for Block C

(4) 4" x wof strips. From the strips, cut:

   (44) 2-1/2" x 4" rectangles for Connecting Blocks and

   (40) 1-1/2" x 4" rectangles for Connecting Blocks

(1) 4" x wof strip. From the strip, cut:

   (18) 1-1/2" x 4" rectangles for

   Half-Connecting Blocks

(7) 2" x wof strips. Sew the strips together along the
   short ends to make one continuous strip.
   From the strip, cut:

   (5) 2" x 48-1/2" sashing strips

(6) 2" x wof strips. Sew the strips together along the
   short ends to make one continuous strip.
   From the strip, cut:

   (2) 2" x 48-1/2" top/bottom border strips

   (2) 2" x 59" side border strips

From light blue fabric, cut:

(6) 2-1/4" x wof binding strips

Block Assembly

Block B

1. Sew a 2-1/2" x 4-1/2" white tonal rectangle to opposite sides of a 4-1/2" light or medium blue square. Press to make a white/blue Block B. Make a total of 12 white/blue Block B.

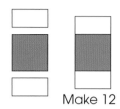

Make 12

2. In the same manner, sew a 2-1/2" x 4-1/2" gray crackle rectangle to opposite sides of a 4-1/2" light or medium blue square. Press to make a gray/blue Block B. Make a total of 14 gray/blue Block B.

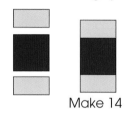

Make 14

Block C

1. Sew a 2" x 4-1/2" dark blue rectangle to opposite sides of a 1-1/2" x 4-1/2" white tonal rectangle.

2. In the same manner, sew a 2-1/2" x 4-1/2" white tonal rectangle to the top and bottom of the sewn unit in step 1. Press to make a Block C. Make a total of 11 Block C.

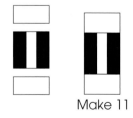

Make 11

Connecting Block D

Sew a 2-1/2" x 4" white tonal rectangle to the opposite sides of a 1-1/2" x 2-1/2" dark blue rectangle to complete Connecting Block D. Make a total of 22 Connecting Block D.

Make 22

Connecting Block E

Sew a 1-1/2" x 4" white tonal rectangle and a 1-1/2" x 4" gray crackle rectangle together along one long edge. Repeat to make 2 units. Sew the units to opposite sides of a 1-1/2" x 2-1/2" dark blue rectangle. Press to complete Connecting Block E. Make a total of 20 Connecting Block E.

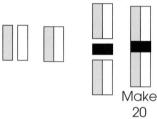

Make 20

Half-Connecting Blocks

1. Sew a 1-1/2" x 4" gray crackle rectangle to opposite sides of a 1-1/2" dark blue square. Press to complete a gray/blue Half-Connecting Block. Make a total of 3 gray/blue Half-Connecting Blocks.

Make 3

2. In the same manner, sew a 1-1/2" x 4" white tonal rectangle to opposite sides of a 1-1/2" dark blue square. Press to make a white/blue Half-Connecting Block. Make a total of 9 white/blue Half-Connecting Blocks.

Make 9

Quilt Top Assembly

1. Referring to the Quilt Center Assembly Diagram, lay out the blocks, connecting blocks, half-connecting blocks and the white tonal 2" x 48-1/2" sashing strips in rows as shown.

2. Sew the pieces together in each row.

3. Sew a sashing strip to the top of rows 2 through 6.

4. Sew the rows together to complete the quilt center.

5. Sew a 2" x 48-1/2" white tonal top/bottom border strip to the top and bottom of the quilt center.

6. Sew a 2" x 59" white tonal side border strip to opposite sides of the quilt center to complete the quilt top.

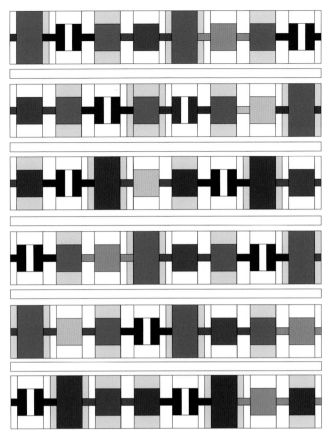

Quilt Top Assembly Diagram

Finishing

1. Lay the backing fabric, wrong side up on a flat surface. The backing fabric should be taut. Layer batting and quilt top, right side up, on top of backing to form a quilt sandwich. Baste the quilt sandwich.

2. Quilt as desired.

3. Sew the (6) 2-1/4" x wof binding strips together along the short ends to make one continuous binding strip. Fold the piece in half lengthwise, wrong sides together, and press. Sew to the raw edge of the quilt top. Fold the binding over the raw edges and hand stitch in place on back of quilt.

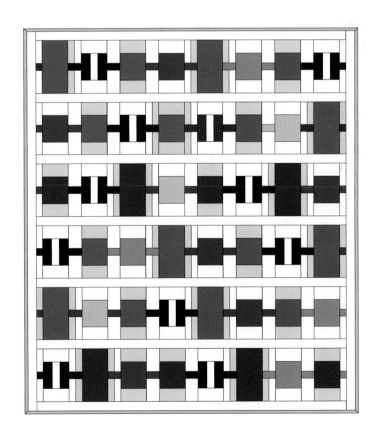

Care for a Cuppa?
WALLHANGING

Designed, pieced and quilted by Wendy Sheppard
Finished block size: 6-1/2"
Finished wallhanging size approximately: 40" square

Materials

Note: I used a precut 10" layer cake and jelly roll bundle from Moda's Winterberry fabric line.

(40) 10" squares assorted light to dark print fabric
    (separate the squares into light, medium
    and dark groups)

(4) 2-1/2" x wof assorted medium gray print fabric strips

(4) 2-1/2" x wof assorted red print fabric strips

(10-12) 2-1/2" x wof assorted light print fabric strips

1/2 yard light taupe polka dot fabric

1/4 yard light fabric

(5) 2-1/2" x wof binding strips

46" square backing fabric

46" square batting

Layer Cake = 10" square
Jelly Roll strip = 2-1/2" x wof
wof = width of fabric
Sew with 1/4" seam allowance unless otherwise noted.

Cutting Instructions

From light print 10" squares, cut:

(9) 7" squares for appliqué block backgrounds

From medium to dark print 10" squares, cut:

(22) 3" squares for inner border 2
Appliqué shapes using the templates on page 29

    (9) cups
    (9) saucers
    (1) small steam
    (1) large steam
    (3) s
    (2) e
    (1) p
    (1) r
    (1) o

From assorted medium gray print strips, cut:

(2) 2-1/2" x 32-1/2" inner border 3 strips
(2) 2-1/2" x 36-1/2" inner border 3 strips

From assorted red print strips, cut:

(2) 2-1/2" x 36-1/2" outer border strips
(2) 2-1/2" x 40-1/2" outer border strips

From assorted light print strips, cut:

(44) 1-1/4" x 3" inner border 2 rectangles
(44) 1-1/4" x 4-1/2" inner border 2 rectangles
(1) 1-1/2" x 4-1/2" inner border 1 rectangle

From light taupe polka dot fabric, cut:

(2) 1-3/4" x wof strips.
    From the strips, cut:
        (6) 1-3/4" x 7" sashing rectangles
(2) 1-3/4" x wof strips.
    From the strips, cut:
        (2) 1-3/4" x 22-1/2" sashing strips
(4) 1-1/2" x wof strips.
    From the strips, cut:
        (2) 1-1/2" x 22-1/2" side inner border 1 strips
        (1) 1-1/2" x 24-1/2" bottom inner border 1 strip
        (1) 1-1/2" x 18-1/2" top inner border 1 strip
        (1) 1-1/2" x 2-1/2" top inner border 1 rectangle

From light fabric, cut:

(2) 4-1/2" x 12-1/2" inner border 2 rectangle

Appliqué Block Assembly

Prepare the appliqué shapes using your favorite method. Fusible appliqué was used on the wallhanging. Referring to the diagram and the photo on page 26, arrange the cup and saucer appliqué pieces on the 7" background blocks. Sew the pieces in place using a favorite appliqué stitch. Make 9 appliqué blocks.

Wallhanging Center Assembly

1. Lay out 3 appliqué blocks and (2) 1-3/4" x 7" light taupe polka dot sashing rectangles in a row. Sew the pieces together to make a row. Make a total of 3 block rows.

2. Lay out the 3 block rows and 1-3/4" x 22-1/2" light taupe polka dot sashing strips. Sew the pieces together to complete the wallhanging center.

Border Assembly

1. Sew 1-1/2" x 22-1/2" light taupe polka dot side inner border 1 strips to opposite sides of the wallhanging center. Sew the 1-1/2" x 24-1/2" light taupe polka dot bottom inner border 1 strip to the bottom of the wallhanging center.

2. Sew the 1-1/2" x 18-1/2" light taupe polka dot top inner border 1 rectangle, 1-1/2" x 4-1/2" light top inner border 1 rectangle and 1-1/2" x 2-1/2" light taupe polka dot top inner border 1 rectangle together to make a top inner border 1 strip. Sew the strip to the top of wallhanging center.

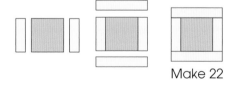

3. Sew 1-1/4" x 3" light inner border 2 rectangles to opposite sides of a 3" medium to dark print square. Sew 1-1/4" x 4-1/2" light inner border 2 rectangles to the remaining sides of the square to complete a unit. Make a total of 22 units.

Make 22

4. Sew 6 units together in a row. Sew the row to the left side of the wallhanging center.

5. Sew 3 units and a 4-1/2" x 12-1/2" light inner border 2 rectangle into a row. Sew the row to the right side of the wallhanging center.

6. Sew 8 units together in a row. Sew the row to the bottom of the wallhanging center.

7. Sew 5 units and a 4-1/2" x 12-1/2" light inner border 2 rectangle into a row. Sew the row to the top of the wallhanging center.

8. Sew 2-1/2" x 32-1/2" gray inner border 3 strips to opposite sides of the wallhanging center. Sew 2-1/2" x 36-1/2" gray inner border 3 strips to the remaining sides of the wallhanging center.

9. Sew 2-1/2" x 36-1/2" red inner border 4 strips to opposite sides of the wallhanging center. Sew 2-1/2" x 40-1/2" red inner border 4 strips to the remaining sides of the wallhanging center to complete the wallhanging top.

10. Prepare the appliqué steam and letter shapes using your favorite method. Fusible appliqué was used on the wallhanging. Referring to the photo on page 26, arrange the appliqué pieces on the top right of border 2. Sew the pieces in place using a favorite appliqué stitch.

Finishing

1. Lay the backing fabric, wrong side up on a flat surface. The backing fabric should be taut. Layer batting and quilt top, right side up, on top of backing to form a quilt sandwich. Baste the quilt sandwich.

2. Quilt as desired.

   Quilting notes: *Appliqué blocks are quilted with background McTavishing motif; border is quilted with informal feathers in contrasting colors.*

3. Sew the (5) 2-1/2" x wof binding strips together along the short ends to make one continuous binding strip. Fold the piece in half lengthwise, wrong sides together, and press. Sew to the raw edge of the quilt top. Fold the binding over the raw edges and hand stitch in place on back of quilt.

Cup
Template

Saucer
Template

Large Steam
Template

Small Steam
Template

Templates have
been reversed for
fusible appliqué

Counting My Blessings
BANNER

Designed, pieced and quilted by Wendy Sheppard
Finished banner size approximately: 18" x 24"

Materials

Note: I used an assortment of batik pops and snaps from Hoffman Fabrics.

Assorted 2-1/2" x wof pastel batik strips

Assorted 5" batik squares

5 assorted 2-1/2" x wof blue and gray batik strips

24" x 30" backing fabric

24" x 30" batting

(3) 2-1/2" x wof binding strips

Pop = 2-1/2" x wof
Snap = 5" square
wof = width of fabric
Sew with 1/4" seam allowance unless otherwise noted.

Cutting Instructions

From assorted 2-1/2" x wof pastel batik strips, cut:

(3) 2-1/2" x 8" strips
(2) 2-1/2" x 10" strips
(3) 2-1/2" x 12" strips
(2) 2-1/2" x 14" strips
(3) 2-1/2" x 16" strips
(2) 2-1/2" x 18" strips
(3) 2-1/2" x 20" strips

From assorted 5" batik squares, cut:
Birdhouse, birdhouse base and birdhouse roof appliqué
    shapes using the templates on page 33
6 circles using the large yo-yo template on page 33
20 circles using the small yo-yo template on page 33

Banner Assembly

1. Referring to the diagram, sew the assorted batik 2-1/2"-wide strips together on the diagonal as shown.

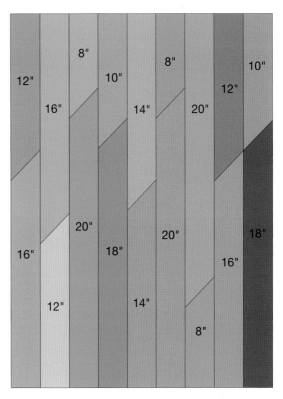

2. Sew the 5 assorted blue and gray batik 2-1/2" x wof strips together along the long edges to make a strip panel. Using the templates on pages 34-35, cut the branch appliqué shapes from the strip panel.

3. Prepare all appliqué shapes using your favorite method. Fusible appliqué was used on the banner. Referring to the diagram on page 32 and the photo on page 30, arrange the appliqué pieces on the pieced background. Sew the pieces in place using a favorite appliqué stitch.

Making the Yo-Yos

1. Finger-press the edges of the assorted batik fabric circles a scant 1/8" to the wrong side of the fabric. Make running stitches close to the fold using one strand of thread.

31

2. Pull the strand of thread tight to create a gathered circle on the right side of the fabric. The back of the yo-yo should be flat. Knot the thread and bury it in the fold of the yo-yo. The large finished yo-yos should measure 1-3/4" in diameter. The small ones should measure 1-1/4" in diameter. Set the yo-yos aside.

Finishing

1. Lay the backing fabric, wrong side up on a flat surface. The backing fabric should be taut. Layer batting and banner top, right side up, on top of backing to form a quilt sandwich. Baste the quilt sandwich.

2. Quilt as desired.

   Quilting notes: *The featured banner is quilted with an allover feather quilting.*

3. Referring to the diagram or the photo on page 30, pin the yo-yos in place and blind stitch to secure to the top of banner. Fabric glue can also be used to hold the yo-yos in place before blind stitching.

4. Square up the banner. Sew the (3) 2-1/2" x wof binding strips together along the short ends to make one continuous binding strip. Fold the piece in half lengthwise, wrong sides together, and press. Sew to the raw edge of the banner top. Fold the binding over the raw edges and hand stitch in place on back of banner.

Fall Color Option

Follow the Counting My Blessings directions and use a darker selection of batiks to make the fall banner. Cut 10 leaf shapes using the template on page 33. The color option uses black charm squares for the shadow pieces. Offset the black leaf appliqué pieces underneath the colored leaf pieces to create a shadow effect. The banner is quilted with a Sand Dunes motif that can be found at https://ivoryspring.wordpress.com/2015/02/18/thread-talk-from-my-sewing-machine-61/.

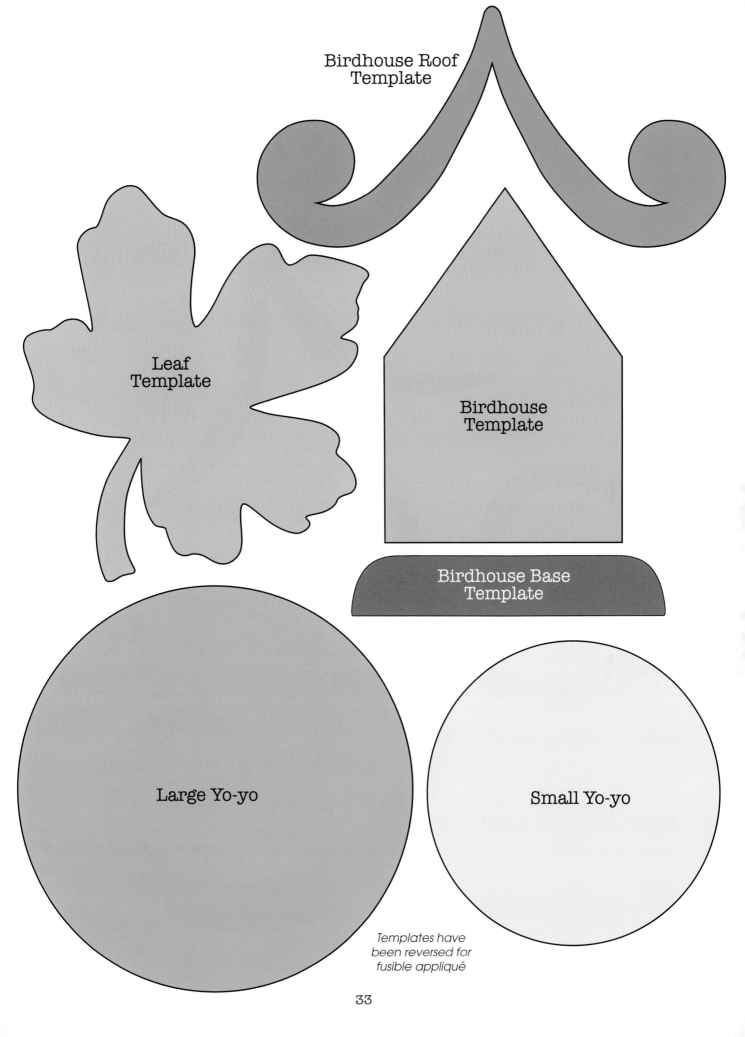

Birdhouse Roof
Template

Leaf
Template

Birdhouse
Template

Birdhouse Base
Template

Large Yo-yo

Small Yo-yo

*Templates have
been reversed for
fusible appliqué*

33

Branch
Template

*Templates have
been reversed for
fusible appliqué*

Branch
Template

*Templates have
been reversed for
fusible appliqué*

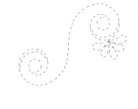

Gwendolyn's Dream Garden
QUILT

Designed by Wendy Sheppard, pieced by Sherry McConnell and quilted by Darlene Szabo
Finished block size: 12" square
Finished quilt size approximately: 78" x 90"

Materials

Note: I used fabrics from the Hello Darling collection by Moda. The design is perfect for using leftover precuts or an assortment of fabrics from your stash.

5 or more assorted fat quarters **OR**
   (72) 5" charm squares for Block A

(33) 2-1/2" x wof white solid strips for Blocks A and B **OR** Jelly Roll bundle of white strips

40 or more 2-1/2" x wof assorted print strips for Blocks A and B **OR** Jelly Roll bundle of assorted prints

28 or more assorted print fat quarters **OR**
   (62) 10" squares for Block B

1-7/8 yards white solid fabric for sashing and border strips

(10) 2-1/2" x wof print strips for binding

84" x 96" backing fabric

84" x 96" batting fabric

wof = width of fabric
Sew with 1/4" seam allowance unless otherwise noted.
Read through all instructions before beginning this project.

Cutting Instructions

From 5 or more assorted fat quarters OR (72) 5" charm squares, cut:

(72) 4-1/2" squares for Block A

Note: 18 sets of matching 4-1/2" squares were used in the featured quilt.

From 12 white solid 2-1/2" x wof strips, cut:

(180) 2-1/2" squares for Block A

From 4 white solid 2-1/2" x wof strips, cut:

(68) 2" squares for Block B

From 13 white solid 2-1/2" x wof strips, cut:

(204) 2-1/2" squares for Block B half-square triangle units

From 12 or more assorted print 2-1/2" x wof strips, cut:

(180) 2-1/2" print squares for Block A

From 28 or more assorted print 2-1/2" x wof strips, cut:

(221) 2-1/2" squares for Block B

(34) 2" x 6-1/2" rectangles for Block B

(34) 2" x 9-1/2" rectangles for Block B

From 28 or more assorted print fat quarters OR
(62) 10" squares, cut:

(17) 1-1/2" x 2-1/2" rectangles for Block B

(34) 1-1/2" x 3-1/2" rectangles for Block B

(34) 1-1/2" x 4-1/2" rectangles for Block B

(34) 1-1/2" x 5-1/2" rectangles for Block B

(17) 1-1/2" x 6-1/2" rectangles for Block B

From white solid fabric, cut:

(17) 3-1/2" x wof strips. Sew the strips together along the short ends to make one continuous strip.
   From the strip, cut:
   (4) 3-1/2" x 84-1/2" sashing strips
   (2) 3-1/2" x 78-1/2" top/bottom border strips
   (2) 3-1/2" x 84-1/2" side border strips

Block Assembly

Block A

1. Lay out (2) 2-1/2" white solid and (2) 2-1/2" assorted print squares as shown. Sew the squares together to make a four-patch unit. Make 5 four-patch units.

Make 5

2. Lay out 5 four-patch units and (4) 4-1/2" squares as shown. Sew the pieces together to complete Block A. Make 18 Block A.

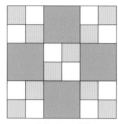

Make 18

Block B

1. Draw a diagonal line on the wrong side of a 2-1/2" assorted print square. With right sides together, place the marked square on a 2-1/2" white solid square. Stitch 1/4" on either side of the drawn line.

2. Cut on drawn line. Press open to make 2 half-square triangle units. Make 24 half-square triangle units. Line up the diagonal seam of the half-square triangle units with the 45-degree line on a ruler. Trim the units to 2" square. Make 24 half-square triangle units.

 Make 24

3. Lay out a 1-1/2" x 2-1/2" print rectangle and a 2-1/2" print square as shown. Sew the pieces together.

4. Sew a 1-1/2" x 3-1/2" print rectangle to the top of the unit in step 3. Sew a 1-1/2" x 3-1/2" print rectangle to the left side of the unit.

5. Sew a 1-1/2" x 4-1/2" print rectangle to the bottom of the unit in step 4.

6. Continuing in a counter-clockwise direction, sew a 1-1/2" x 4-1/2" print rectangle, (2) 1-1/2" x 5-1/2" print rectangles and a 1-1/2" x 6-1/2" print rectangle to the sewn unit.

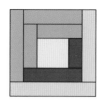

7. Sew 2" x 6-1/2" print rectangles to opposite sides of the sewn unit. Sew 2" x 9-1/2" print rectangles to the remaining sides of the sewn unit to complete a Block B center.

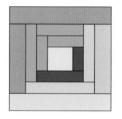

8. Lay out 6 half-square triangle units in a row. Sew the units together to make a column. Make 4 columns.

9. Sew 2 columns to opposite sides of the Block B center.

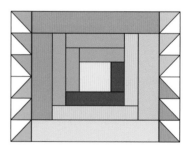

10. Sew a 2" white solid square to the opposite sides of the remaining columns. Sew the columns to the top and bottom of the Block B center to complete Block B. Make a total of 17 Block B.

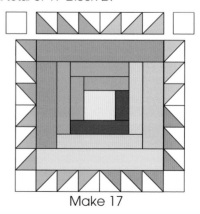

Make 17

Quilt Top Assembly

1. Referring to the Quilt Center Assembly Diagram, lay out blocks A and B in 5 columns as shown.

2. Sew the blocks together in columns.

3. Lay out the 5 columns and (4) 3-1/2" x 84-1/2" sashing strips as shown.

4. Sew the pieces together to complete the quilt top center.

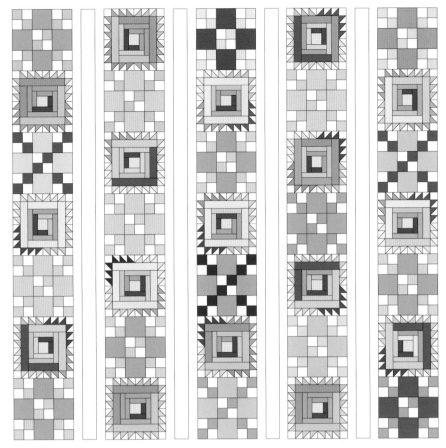

Quilt Center Assembly Diagram

5. Sew 3-1/2" x 84-1/2" side border strips to opposite sides of the quilt center.

6. Sew 3-1/2" x 78-1/2" top/bottom border strips to the top/bottom of the quilt center to complete the quilt top.

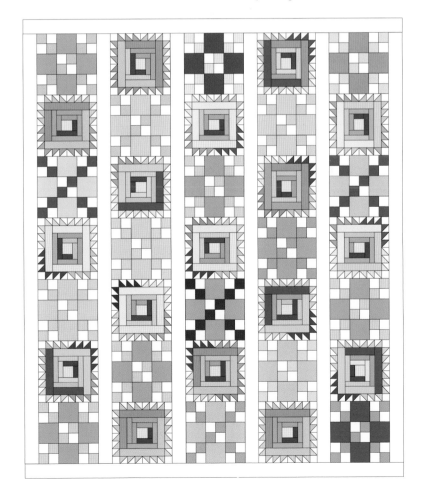

Finishing

1. Lay the backing fabric, wrong side up on a flat surface. The backing fabric should be taut. Place the batting on the backing and the quilt top on the batting, right side up, to form a quilt sandwich. Baste the quilt sandwich.

2. Quilt as desired.

   Quilting notes: *Allover swirl/petal motifs were quilted over the entire quilt top.*

3. Sew the (10) 2-1/2" x wof binding strips together along the short ends to make one continuous binding strip. Fold the piece in half lengthwise, wrong sides together, and press. Sew to the raw edge of the quilt top. Fold the binding over the raw edges and hand stitch in place on back of quilt.

Stars Over Columbia
QUILT

Designed, pieced and quilted by Wendy Sheppard
Finished block size: 9" square
Finished quilt size approximately: 36" x 45"

Materials

Note: I used my stash to precut the following pieces. For a really scrappy look use lots of different fabrics. You can also use an assortment of 5" charm squares. See "From Wendy" below.

From Wendy: I cut all my pieces into 5" squares using my stash. I then trimmed away the excess to create the size squares needed for the project. By doing this, I feel I can achieve better accuracy with my half-square and quarter-square triangles.

(18) 3-1/2" squares assorted blue fabric

(2) 3-1/2" squares assorted red fabric

(7) 4" squares assorted red fabric

(40) 4" squares assorted light and dark gray/taupe fabric

(4) 4-1/2" squares assorted red fabric

(36) 4-1/2" squares assorted light and dark blue fabric

(40) 4-1/2" squares assorted light gray/taupe fabric

(5) 2-1/2" x wof strips assorted taupe fabric for binding

40" x 50" backing fabric

40" x 50" batting

wof = width of fabric
Sew with 1/4" seam allowance unless otherwise noted.

Unit Assembly
Half-square triangle units

1. Draw a diagonal line on the wrong side of a 4" light gray/taupe square. With right sides together, place the marked square on a 4" dark gray/taupe square.

2. Stitch 1/4" on both sides of the drawn line.

3. Cut on the drawn line. Press open to make 2 light/dark gray/taupe half-square triangle units.

4. Trim the units to 3-1/2" square by matching the 45-degree seam of the half-square triangles to the 45-degree line of the ruler.

5. Make a total of 66 light/dark gray/taupe half-square triangle units and 14 red/gray/taupe half-square triangle units.

Make 66   Make 14

Quarter-square triangle units

1. Draw a diagonal line on the wrong side of a 4-1/2" light gray/taupe square. With right sides together, place the marked square on a 4-1/2" blue square.

2. Stitch 1/4" on both sides of the drawn line.

3. Cut on the drawn line. Press open to make 2 blue/light gray/taupe half-square triangle units.

4. Make a total of 72 blue/light gray/taupe half-square triangle units.

5. Draw a diagonal line on the wrong side of a half-square triangle unit from step 4. With right sides together and opposite colors matching, place the marked unit on another unit from step 4.

6. Stitch 1/4" on both sides of the drawn line.

7. Cut on the drawn line. Press open to make 2 blue/light gray/taupe quarter-square triangle units. The units should measure 3-1/2" square.

8. Make a total of 72 blue/light gray/taupe quarter-square triangle units and 8 red/light gray/taupe quarter-square triangle units.

Make 72   Make 8

Star Block Assembly

1. Sew a light/dark gray/taupe half-square triangle unit to opposite sides of a blue/light gray/taupe quarter-square triangle unit to make row A. Make 2 row A.

Make 2

2. Sew a blue/light gray/taupe quarter-square triangle unit to opposite sides of 3 1/2" blue square to make row B.

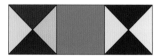

3. Sew rows A and B together to make a blue star block. Make 12 blue star blocks.

Make 12

4. Following steps 1-3, make 6 blue/red star blocks and 2 red star blocks.

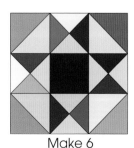 

Make 6   Make 2

Quilt Top Assembly

1. Referring to the Quilt Top Assembly Diagram, lay out the blocks in 5 rows with 4 blocks in each row as shown.

2. Sew the blocks together in each row. Sew the rows together to complete the quilt top.

Quilt Top Assembly Diagram

Finishing

1. Lay the backing fabric, wrong side up on a flat surface. The backing fabric should be taut. Place the batting on the backing and the quilt top on the batting, right side up, to form a quilt sandwich. Baste the quilt sandwich.

2. Quilt as desired.

   Quilting notes: An allover sand dunes motif was quilted over the entire quilt top. See Tips on Quilting a Borderless Quilt on page 45.

3. Sew the (5) 2-1/2" x wof binding strips together along the short ends to make one continuous binding strip. Fold the piece in half lengthwise, wrong sides together, and press. Sew to the raw edge of the quilt top. Fold the binding over the raw edges and hand stitch in place on back of quilt.

Tips on Quilting Borderless Quilts

When quilting borderless quilts, it is important to have your pieced quilt top squared up and flat even before quilting. Here are a few tips:

- If possible, use batiks since these fabrics have a higher thread count than regular cotton. It will help maintain the square-ness of the quilt. When using regular cotton fabrics, make sure to starch the fabrics and block patches during the construction process.

- Use a lightweight cotton batting. The cotton batting and fabric pieces seem to naturally adhere to each other preventing unintended shifting during the quilting process.

- Pin baste the quilt sandwich before quilting. I also trim my batting and backing even with the quilt top, and then zigzag around the quilt corners with a loose zigzag stitch. This tends to keep the corners from getting wonky and being pulled in the quilting process.

- Choose a simple quilting scheme that is quilted with even density. It won't require pulling and scrunching the quilt in all directions while quilting.

Childhood Memories
QUILT

Designed, pieced and quilted by Wendy Sheppard
Finished block size: 18" square
Finished quilt size approximately: 36" x 45"

From Wendy: This design is a perfect way to use any 18" square orphan blocks.
If your block doesn't measure 18" square, add strips to increase the size.

Materials

Note: This project is a good way to use leftover jelly roll strips. Jelly roll strips need to be a minimum of 42" long for the featured quilt. If your jelly roll strips are shorter, you will need 13 assorted print strips instead of 12.

(12) 2-1/2" x wof assorted print strips

(1) 2-1/2" x wof solid white strip

(2) yellow print fat quarters

(2) blue print fat quarters

(2) pink print fat quarters

(1) brown print fat quarter

(5) 2-1/2" x wof strips for binding

42" x 50" backing fabric

42" x 50" batting

Jelly roll strip = 2-1/2" x wof

wof = width of fabric

Sew with 1/4" seam allowance unless otherwise noted.

Cutting Instructions

From 9 assorted print strips, cut:
(4) 2-1/2" x 10-1/2" rectangles from each strip
    for a total of 36 rectangles

From 3 assorted print strips, cut:
(3) 2-1/2" x 36-1/2" sashing strips

From the white solid strip, cut:
(2) 1" x 36-1/2" sashing strips

From 1 of *each* yellow, blue and pink print fat quarters, cut:
(1) 4-1/2" x 6-1/2" rectangle
(1) 6-1/2" x 14-1/2" rectangle

From remaining yellow print fat quarter, cut:
(4) 2" squares
(4) 2-1/2" squares
(3) 2-1/2" x 4-1/2" rectangles

From remaining blue print fat quarter, cut:
(6) 2-1/2" squares
(2) 4-1/2" x 6-1/2" rectangles
(1) 2-1/2" x 6-1/2" rectangle

From remaining pink print fat quarter, cut:
(2) 2-1/2" x 4-1/2" rectangles
(1) 6-1/2" x 14-1/2" rectangle

From brown print fat quarter, cut:
(1) 2-1/2" square
(2) 2-1/2" x 8-1/2" rectangles
(4) 2-1/2" x 6-1/2" rectangles
(8) 2-1/2" x 4-1/2" rectangles

Block Assembly

1. Sew a 2-1/2" x 4-1/2" brown print rectangle to opposite sides of a 2-1/2" x 4-1/2" yellow print rectangle as shown to make Unit A. Make 2 Unit A.

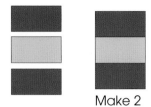

Make 2

2. Draw a diagonal line on the wrong side of the 2-1/2" yellow print squares. With right sides together, place one marked square on a corner of a 2-1/2" x 6-1/2" brown print rectangle.

3. Stitch on the drawn line. Trim 1/4" away from sewn line. Press open to reveal the yellow corner triangle. Repeat on the other end of the brown print rectangle to complete Unit B. Make 2 Unit B.

Make 2

4. Sew Unit B to the right side of Unit A. Carefully watch the orientation of Unit B. Make 2.

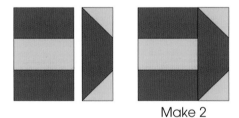

Make 2

5. Draw a diagonal line on the wrong side of the 2" yellow print squares. With right sides together, place one marked square on a corner of a 2-1/2" x 6-1/2" brown print rectangle. Stitch on the drawn line. Trim 1/4" away from sewn line. Press open to reveal the yellow corner triangle. Repeat on the other end of the brown print rectangle to complete Unit C. Make 2 Unit C.

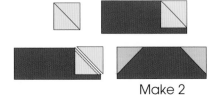

Make 2

6. Sew Unit C to the left side of the unit in step 4. Carefully watch the orientation of Unit C. Make 2.

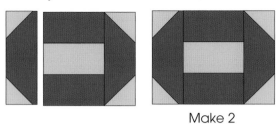

Make 2

7. Draw a diagonal line on the wrong side of the 2-1/2" blue print squares. With right sides together, place one marked square on a corner of a 2-1/2" x 4-1/2" brown print rectangle.

8. Stitch on the drawn line. Trim 1/4" away from sewn line. Press open to reveal the blue corner triangle to complete Unit D. Repeat to make another Unit D the mirror image of the first.

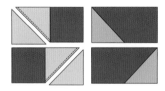

9. Sew Unit D to the right side of one 4-1/2" x 6-1/2" blue print rectangle and to the left side of the other 4-1/2" x 6-1/2" blue print rectangle. Carefully watch the orientation of Unit D.

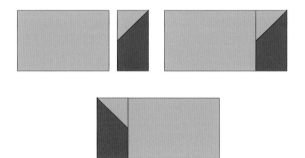

10. Draw a diagonal line on the wrong side of the 2-1/2" blue print squares. With right sides together, place one marked square on a corner of a 2-1/2" x 8-1/2" brown print rectangle.

11. Stitch on the drawn line. Trim 1/4" away from sewn line. Press open to reveal the blue corner triangle. Repeat on the other end of the brown print rectangle sewing the second blue print square parallel to the first one. Press open to complete Unit E. Make 2 Unit E.

Make 2

12. Sew Unit E to the units made in step 9.

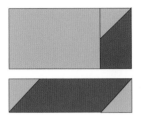 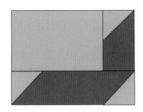

13. Sew the step 6 and step 12 units together as shown. The 2" corner triangles are on the outside of the unit. Repeat to make another unit the mirror image of the first.

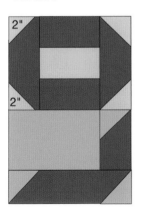 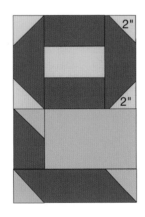

14. Sew a 2-1/2" x 4-1/2" yellow print rectangle, 2-1/2" brown print square and 2-1/2" x 6-1/2" blue print rectangle together in a column as shown.

15. Sew the column and units from step 13 together as shown to complete the top section of the block.

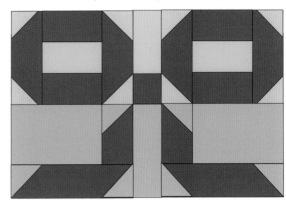

16. Sew the 2-1/2" x 4-1/2" pink print rectangles and 2-1/2" x 4-1/2" brown print rectangles together using diagonal seams as shown. One should be the mirror image of the other.

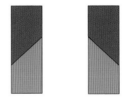

17. Sew the units from step 16 to opposite sides of the 6-1/2" x 14-1/2" pink print rectangle to complete the bottom section of the block.

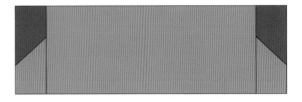

18. Sew the top and bottom block sections together to complete the block.

Quilt Top Assembly

1. Lay out (18) 2-1/2" x 10-1/2" assorted print rectangles in a horizontal row. Sew the rectangles together to make a pieced strip. Make 2 pieced strips.

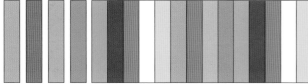

Make 2

2. Lay out the yellow, blue and pink print 6-1/2" x 14-1/2" rectangles in a column as shown. Sew the rectangles together to make column A.

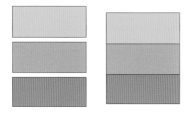

3. Lay out the yellow, blue and pink print 4-1/2" x 6-1/2" rectangles in a column as shown. Sew the rectangles together to make column B.

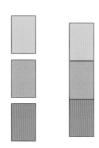

4. Lay out column A, the block and column B as shown. Sew the pieces together to complete the quilt top center section.

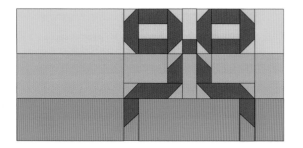

5. Referring to the Quilt Top Assembly Diagram, lay out the pieced strips, quilt top center section and sashing strips as shown.

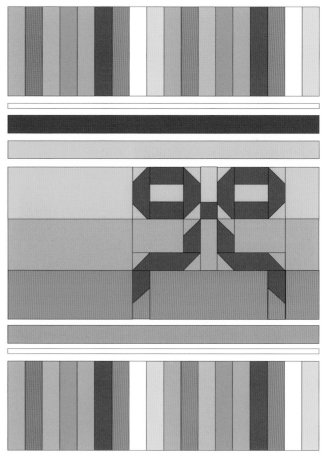

Quilt Top Assembly Diagram

Finishing

1. Lay the backing fabric, wrong side up on a flat surface. The backing fabric should be taut. Place the batting on the backing and the quilt top on the batting, right side up, to form a quilt sandwich. Baste the quilt sandwich.

2. Quilt as desired.

   Quilting notes: *A swirly vine with variations was used on the featured quilt. For an example of the quilting visit https://ivoryspring.wordpress.com/2011/07/07/thread-talk-from-my-sewing-machine-21/*

3. Sew the (5) 2-1/2" x wof binding strips together along the short ends to make one continuous binding strip. Fold the piece in half lengthwise, wrong sides together, and press. Sew to the raw edge of the quilt top. Fold the binding over the raw edges and hand stitch in place on back of quilt.

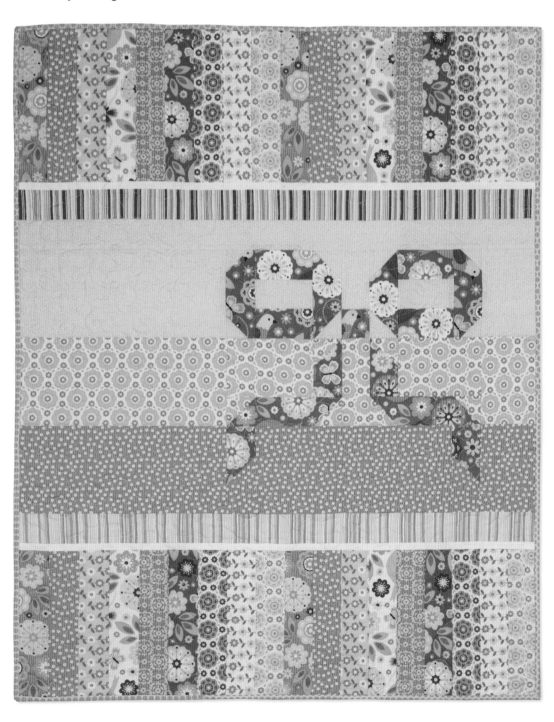

Optional Block for Childhood Memories Quilt

Sailboat Block

Materials

(1) orange stripe fat quarter

(1) blue stripe fat quarter

(1) blue print fat quarter

(1) floral print fat quarter **OR**
   (1) 1-1/2" x 13-1/2" scrap piece

(1) tree print fat quarter

Fat quarter = 18" x 22"

Cutting Instructions

Note: If you are using a directional print fabric similar to the stripe fabric used in the sailboat block, pay special attention when cutting the fabric.

From orange stripe fat quarter, cut:

(2) 9-1/4" x 12" rectangles.

   Cut each rectangle in half diagonally to make
   4 half-rectangle triangles. Choose two half-rectangles
   with stripes going in same direction for the block.
Note: If print fabric isn't directional, you will only need one 9-1/4" x 12" rectangle.

(2) 1-1/2" x 9" rectangles

(1) 2-1/2" x 9" rectangle

(2) 3-1/2" squares

From blue stripe fat quarter, cut:

(1) 9-1/4" x 12" rectangle.

   Cut the rectangle in half diagonally to make
   2 half-rectangle triangles. You will only need one.

From blue print fat quarter, cut:

(1) 9-1/4" x 12" rectangle.

   Cut the rectangle in half diagonally to make
   2 half-rectangle triangles. You will only need one.

(1) 2-1/2" x 18-1/2" rectangle

From floral print fat quarter, cut:

(1) 1-1/2" x 13-1/2" rectangle

From tree print fat quarter, cut:

(1) 3-1/2" x 18-1/2" rectangle

Block Assembly

1. Layer an orange stripe half-rectangle triangle and a blue print half-rectangle triangle, right sides together. Sew the pieces together along the long edge. Press open to make Unit A.

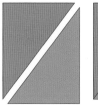

2. Sew a 2-1/2" x 9-1/2" orange stripe rectangle to the bottom of Unit A to make the left section of the block.

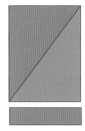 

3. Layer an orange stripe half-rectangle triangle and a blue stripe half-rectangle triangle, right sides together. Sew the pieces together along the long edge. Press open to make Unit B.

4. Sew 1-1/2" x 9-1/2" orange stripe rectangles to the top and bottom of Unit B to make the right section of the block.

5. Sew the left and right sections of the block to opposite sides of the 1-1/2" x 13-1/2" floral print rectangle to complete the block's top section.

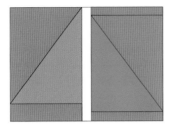

6. Draw a diagonal line on the wrong side of the 3-1/2" orange stripe squares. Pay attention to the direction of the stripes. With right sides together, place a marked square at a corner of a 3-1/2" x 18-1/2" tree print rectangle.

7. Stitch on the drawn line. Trim 1/4" away from sewn line. Press open to reveal the orange stripe corner triangle. Repeat on the other end of the tree print rectangle. Press open to complete Unit C.

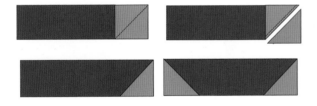

8. Sew a 2-1/2" x 18-1/2" blue print rectangle to the bottom of Unit C to complete the block's bottom section.

9. Sew the top and bottom block sections together to complete the block.

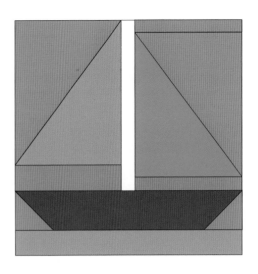

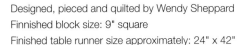

Spring Basket
TABLE RUNNER

Designed, pieced and quilted by Wendy Sheppard

Finnished block size: 9" square

Finished table runner size approximately: 24" x 42"

Materials

Note: I used my stash to precut the following pieces. If you have several candy packs (2-1/2" squares), you can use them to cut the 2-3/8" assorted color squares.

(4) 3-7/8" assorted dark red print squares

(8) 2-3/8" assorted dark red print squares.
 Cut the squares in half once on the diagonal to make 16 small triangles.

(12) 2-3/8" assorted medium red print squares.
 Cut the squares in half once on the diagonal to make 24 small triangles.

(16) 2-3/8" assorted pink print squares.
 Cut the squares in half once on the diagonal to make 32 small triangles.

Assorted green print scraps for basket handles

(62) 2-1/2" assorted pink, medium red, dark red, yellow and green print squares

1 yard white tonal fabric

5/8 yard pink print fabric

28" x 46" backing fabric

28" x 46" batting

wof = width of fabric

Sew with 1/4" seam allowance unless otherwise noted.

Cutting Instructions

From white tonal fabric, cut:

(8) 2" squares

(4) 3-7/8" squares

(16) 2" x 6-7/8" rectangles.
 Cut 8 rectangles at a 45-degree angle going to the right and 8 at a 45-degree angle going to the left.

Make 8   Make 8

(20) 2-3/8" squares.
 Cut the squares in half once on the diagonal to make 40 small triangles.

(4) 9-7/8" squares.
 Cut the squares in half once on the diagonal to make 8 large triangles.

From pink print fabric, cut:

(4) 1-1/2" x wof strips. Sew the strips together along the short ends to make one continuous strip.
 From the strip, cut:
 (2) 1-1/2" x 20-1/2" inner border strips
 (2) 1-1/2" x 36-1/2" inner border strips

(5) 2-1/4" x wof strips for binding

From assorted green print scraps, cut:

8 basket handles using the pattern on page 59

Block Assembly

1. Draw a diagonal line on the wrong side of a 3-7/8" white tonal square. With right sides together, place the marked square on a 3-7/8" dark red square. Stitch 1/4" on either side of the drawn line.

2. Cut on drawn line. Press open to make 2 half-square triangle units. Set one unit aside.

3. Draw a diagonal line on the wrong side of a 2" white tonal square. With right sides together, place the marked square on the dark red side of a half-square triangle unit.

4. Stitch on the drawn line. Trim 1/4" away from sewn line. Press open to make a corner triangle.

5. Lay out 2 white tonal, 1 assorted dark red, 1 assorted medium red and 1 pink print small triangle in a row as shown. Sew the triangles together to make a triangle row.

6. Sew the triangle row and a 2" x 6-7/8" white tonal rectangle together as shown to make a row unit. Sew the row unit and corner triangle together.

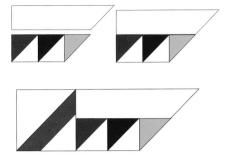

7. Lay out 3 white tonal, 1 assorted dark red, 2 assorted medium red and 3 pink print small triangles in a row as shown. Sew the triangles together in rows. Sew the rows together to make a triangle unit.

 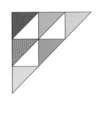

8. Sew the triangle unit and a 2" x 6-7/8" white tonal rectangle together as shown. Sew the pieced unit and unit from step 6 together to complete the bottom of the basket block.

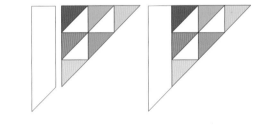

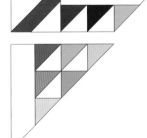 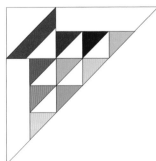

9. Prepare the basket handles using your favorite appliqué method. Machine fusible appliqué was used on the Basket Table Runner. Referring to the diagram for placement, appliqué a basket handle to a large white tonal triangle.

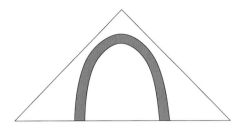

10. Sew the bottom of the basket block and the basket handle portion together to complete a basket block. Make 8 basket blocks.

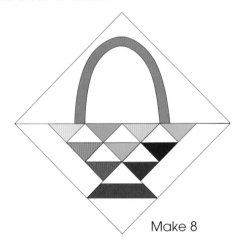

Make 8

Runner Top Assembly

1. Referring to the Runner Top Center Assembly Diagram, lay out the 8 basket blocks in 4 rows with 2 blocks in each row.

2. Sew the blocks together in rows. Sew the rows together to complete the runner center.

Runner Top Center Assembly Diagram

3. Sew 1-1/2" x 36-1/2" pink print inner border strips to opposite long sides of the runner center.

4. Sew 1-1/2" x 20-1/2" pink print inner border strips to the short sides of the runner center.

5. Referring to the Runner Top Assembly Diagram on page 58, lay out 19 assorted print 2-1/2" squares in a column. Sew the squares together to make an outer border column. Make 2 outer border columns.

6. Sew the outer border columns to opposite long sides of the runner.

7. Referring to the Runner Top Assembly Diagram, lay out 12 assorted print 2-1/2" squares in a column. Sew the squares together to make an outer border column. Make 2 outer border columns.

8. Sew the outer border columns to opposite short sides of the runner to complete the runner top.

Finishing

1. Lay the backing fabric, wrong side up on a flat surface. The backing fabric should be taut. Place the batting on the backing and the runner top on the batting, right side up, to form a quilt sandwich. Baste the quilt sandwich.

2. Quilt as desired.

    Quilting notes: *Visit https://ivoryspring.wordpress. com/2015/04/03/thread-talk-from-my-sewing- machine-62/ to see the quilting motif used in the featured runner.*

3. Sew the (5) 2-1/4" x wof binding strips together along the short ends to make one continuous binding strip. Fold the piece in half lengthwise, wrong sides together, and press. Sew to the raw edge of the quilt top. Fold the binding over the raw edges and hand stitch in place on back of quilt.

Runner Top Assembly Diagram

Basket Handle Template

Templates have been reversed for fusible appliqué

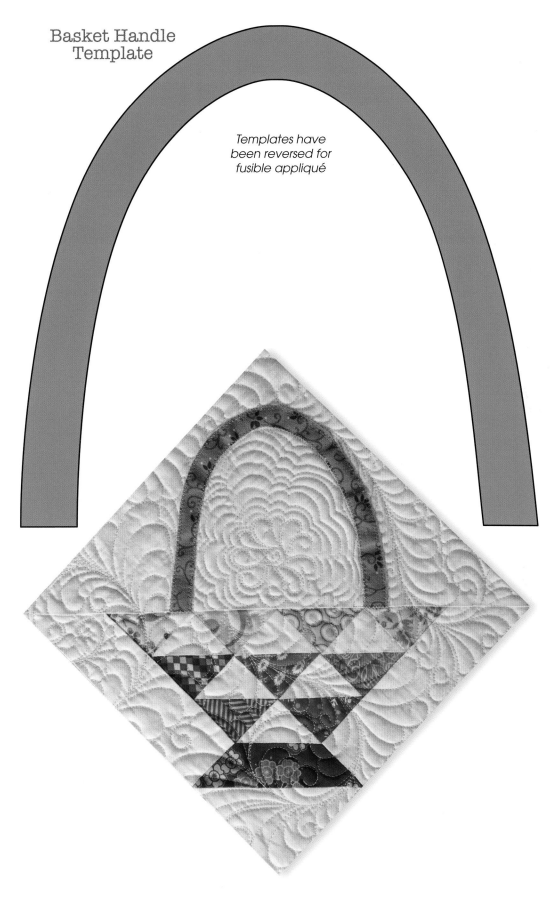

Flight of Colors Pillow

Designed, pieced and quilted by Wendy Sheppard
Finished pillow size approximately: 18" square

Materials

Note: I used the leftover triangles from the Cross Quilt on page 6 and trimmed the short sides to 2-3/8" to make the pillow. The rest of the fabrics were precut from my stash.

1/2 yard light gray tonal fabric

Assortment of (18) 2-3/8" color tonal squares. Cut the squares in half once on the diagonal to make 36 small triangles.

1/8 yard brown tonal fabric

1-1/8 yard pillow backing fabric

22" square batting

22" square pillow top backing fabric
if quilting pillow top before constructing the pillowcase

18" square pillow form

wof = width of fabric
Sew with 1/4" seam allowance unless otherwise noted

Cutting Instructions

From light gray tonal fabric, cut:

(4) 2" squares

(2) 3-7/8" squares

(8) 2" x 6-7/8" rectangles.
   Cut 4 rectangles at a 45-degree angle going to the right and 4 at a 45-degree angle going to the left.

Make 4   Make 4

(10) 2-3/8" squares.
   Cut the squares in half once on the diagonal to make 20 small triangles.

(2) 9-7/8" squares.
   Cut the squares in half once on the diagonal to make 4 large triangles.

From brown tonal fabric, cut:

(2) 3-7/8" squares

From pillow backing fabric, cut:

(2) 18-1/2" squares

Block Assembly

1. Draw a diagonal line on the wrong side of a 3-7/8" light gray tonal square. With right sides together, place the marked square on a 3-7/8" brown tonal square. Stitch 1/4" on either side of the drawn line.

2. Cut on drawn line. Press open to make 2 half-square triangle blocks. Make 4 half-square triangle units.

Make 4

3. Draw a diagonal line on the wrong side of a 2" gray tonal square. With right sides together, place the marked square on the brown tonal side of a half-square triangle unit.

4. Stitch on the drawn line. Trim 1/4" away from sewn line. Press open to make a corner triangle unit. Make 4 corner triangle units.

Make 4

5. Lay out 3 assorted color tonal small triangles and 2 light gray tonal small triangles in a row as shown. Sew the triangles together.

6. Sew the triangle row and a 2" x 6-7/8" light gray tonal rectangle together as shown to make a row unit. Sew the row unit and a corner triangle units together.

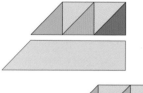 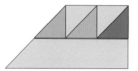

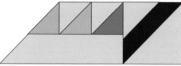

7. Lay out 6 assorted color tonal small triangles and 3 light gray tonal small triangles as shown. Sew the triangles together.

8. Sew the triangle unit and a 2" x 6-7/8" light gray tonal rectangle together as shown.

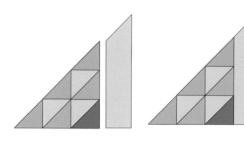

9. Sew the units from step 6 and 8 together to complete a half basket block.

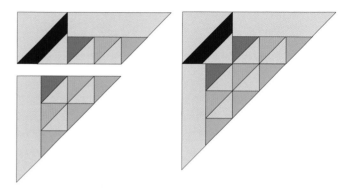

10. Sew a light gray tonal large triangle and a half basket block together to complete a basket block. Referring to the photo on page 63, use the remaining assorted tonal small triangles to make a total of 4 basket blocks.

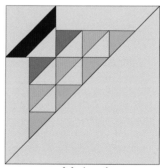

Make 4

Pillow Top Assembly

Lay out the 4 basket blocks as shown. Sew the blocks together to complete the pillow top.

Finishing the Pillow Top

1. Layer the pillow top, batting and pillow top back piece together. Baste the pieces together.

2. Quilt as desired.

   Quilting notes: *I quilted my pillow top before assembling the pillow to give it a bit of a dimensional look. I treated the pillow top as a quilt, to be basted and quilted accordingly.*

3. Trim the pillow to 18-1/2" square.

Finishing the Pillow

1. Turn under 1/4" on one edge of an 18-1/2" pillow back piece. Turn the same edge under again approximately 4". Press. Edge stitch along the outer edges of the flap to hold it in place. Repeat with the remaining 18-1/2" pillow back piece.

2. Place the quilted pillow top right side up on a flat surface. Lay the pillow back pieces on the quilted pillow top, right sides together. Adjust the pillow back pieces as needed, and trim any excess from the 18-1/2" area that is not covering the pillow top.

3. Pin and stitch the pieces together around the outside edge.

   Note: I used a 1/2" seam allowance for a snugger fit, but you may choose to use a 1/4" seam allowance for a looser fit.

4. Trim the corners. Finish by zigzagging the seam allowance to reduce the bulk of all the pieces stitched together.

5. Turn the pillowcase right side out. Press and insert pillow form.

acknowledgments

To Barbara Herring—my quilting teacher, mentor and friend. If she had insisted I make a four-patch beginner quilt for my first project, it's unlikely I would have progressed any further. Instead she patiently and graciously helped me through the intermediate pieced and appliquéd design I had chosen. Over the course of my quilting journey, Barbara remains a constant encourager in my life.

To Rogers Sewing Center—The people at my quilting "mother ship" have been a great source of encouragement and support. I count Dan and Rhonda, of Rogers Sewing Center, two of the dearest people in my life.

To my bloggy friends—Quilters are some of the sweetest people on earth, including the many I have met online through my blog, ivoryspring.wordpress.com. Many of these friendships are forged through late night email exchanges.

To the lovely group at Landauer—This book would not have happened without the very capable editorial team at Landauer Publishing. I have thoroughly enjoyed working with them.

To my sister—She is my most enthusiastic cheerleader and has never seen a quilt of mine she didn't like. She is always available to chat and keep me awake when I work late into the night meeting deadlines.

To my little family—I am appreciative of my husband who is more than supportive in all my quilting endeavors. Without his understanding, this book would not have happened. Despite his own busy schedule, he offered countless times to do school runs and take care of dinner while things got frantically crazy for me. Our daughter is also our family's self-appointed "quilt critic" who gives her honest opinions (a little too) freely regarding my quilts. Sometimes I wonder how I ever made it without my six-year-old's "professional" advice.

To my parents—I owe them for all the adventures I have had in my life. They raised me with the vision to do my best and have sustained me through their faithful prayers.

To my Lord and Savior, apart from Whom I am nothing. I seek to reflect His beauty and glory through my work, albeit a very feeble endeavor on my part. Soli Deo Gloria!

Special Thanks to the following companies for their generosity:

Fabrics: Hoffman Fabrics, Moda, Quilting Treasures, Riley Blake, RJR Fabrics

Threads: Aurifil

Batting: Hobbs

Fusible: Warm Company